T0367861

SWEET
SURRENDER

SALEE DAVIDS

authorHOUSE®

AuthorHouse™ LLC
1663 Liberty Drive
Bloomington, IN 47403
www.authorhouse.com
Phone: 1-800-839-8640

Published by AuthorHouse   10/17/2013

ISBN: 978-1-4817-6725-5 (sc)
ISBN: 978-1-4817-6726-2 (e)

Library of Congress Control Number: 2013911258

DEDICATION

I like to dedicate this book to my heavenly Father my creator, my Savior Lord Jesus Christ, and MY BEST FRIEND the Holy Spirit. I would also like to dedicate it to my parents whom God chose to give me this earthly life. I also dedicate this book to my two sweet daughters, without their love, support and encouragement I couldn't have done it at all. I Love you both so much.

WHO IS THIS BOOK FOR?

This book is for anyone and everyone who is looking for a *happy* life. It doesn't matter how old you are, what gender you are, what your nationality is, or what language you speak. God created everyone. He speaks every language (He created that too). Let me explain. There is a way you can have a PERSONAL relationship with the creator of the universe. You think I'm joking. No, I'm as serious as the sun rises every morning! The relationship is with the One who created the Sun, the Moon, the Stars and everything else. "How is that possible?" you may ask, or you already know about it but didn't think it was for you. Or maybe there was a time in your life when you thought you were going in that direction, but halfway through you gave up because of lack of encouragement when you encountered difficulties. It is never too late. **It's ok, you are in the right place at the right time. Read on** . . . .

INTRODUCTION

The Lord laid it on my heart to write this book over 2 years ago. He gave me the name of the book first. Since I'm involved in ministries in my church, at first I thought that name was something related to a ministry. Then the idea came to my mind to write this book. One day somebody I know with the gift of prophecy was talking to me about writing a book. In the middle of our conversation as we were in my car driving somewhere she said, "The Lord said something about writing a book". However, she didn't make it very clear, other than the Lord said something about writing a book. I responded by saying, "really?" She said "yeah, but I don't know anything about writing".

Right away, the Spirit of God translated it for me. "She is talking about *you* writing the book." Slowly I started writing, but I would say I didn't get the proper anointing till recently. Trust me, it is more or less like God telling me "just do it" and I said "yes, Lord".

God can use each one of you to bring glory and honor to His name. I am trusting in the Lord that this book will go out and get the attention of:

1. Young people: You need to commit your life to Jesus. Read this book and make the decisions regarding your future, whatever they may be. The Holy Spirit (Spirit of God) is your counselor. If you haven't surrendered your life to Jesus, I pray that you will do it, and this book will help you significantly.

2. People who have made mistakes in the past: You made wrong choices, or you even thought you heard from God, but you really didn't hear it right. God is a God of SECOND CHANCES. I trust and pray that sharing my story will encourage you to rethink and recommit your plans to God.

The purpose of writing this book is to tell others how wonderful it is to know, and to have a personal relationship with Almighty God; the creator of heaven and earth and everything in it. God controls everything. He's in charge of everything that happens in the heaven and in the earth. He is the BIG BOSS! But He is also a loving father. His love for us is much stronger than the love of our earthly father and mother, even when they are the best parents in the whole wide world. However, because God is holy and we are not, we can only go to Him through a mediator. God decided who that person was going to be when He sent His only son Jesus Christ to earth, because He loves us so much. Translated into simple English, John3:16 says this: If you accept Jesus as your Lord and saviour He'll call you His child, it's just that He has some rules and regulations. And if you make a mistake, just ask Jesus to bail you out. There's no charge, no fee, except your loyalty. Wow! That's a deal nobody can refuse!!

You can live a life that brings such joy and peace by committing your life to Jesus even at an early age. My prayer is that every young person who doesn't know Jesus yet, or those who have already made the commitment but need more information and guidance, will read this book. You may be saying now, "Stop! Stop! Tell me how do I do this?" Pray this simple prayer. "Jesus I know you came to this world to save sinners. I'm a sinner, I need you in my life, and I accept you as my Lord and Saviour". If you said that simple prayer, you have just become a child of God.

This is a very basic book written in everyday speaking language. The Lord talked to me about writing this book about 2 years ago. I started but never got around to completing it until recently when He really put the pressure on me to do it. Everything I talk about in this book is my own experience, good and bad. I like reading the life experiences of others because I find that it has a more powerful impact on me, than just a fictional story. I made some wrong turns, nothing bad in the natural, but in the eyes of God, I was hurting Him. Even though I didn't purposely try to make God sad, I wasn't loyal to God when I made those choices. I didn't understand the call of God on my life and thus, I made the wrong choices, and I suffered the consequences. Nevertheless, it was never too late to turn around and get back on track again.

How hard is it? How fast can we do it? As fast as we can make a decision to repent (ask God for forgiveness) and He will take us back. Even when our mistakes are harsh and we do shameful things He'll forgive us. He is a merciful God. When we're so down and depressed and even suicidal, He is there. Lamentations 3: 21-23 says, *"yet there is one ray of hope. His compassion never ends. It is only the Lord's mercies that have kept us from complete destruction. Great is His faithfulness, His loving kindness begins afresh each day."* You could be 13 or you could be in your 60's, or older, or anywhere in between. It's never too early or too late to start your journey with Jesus. Having said that, my earnest desire and my prayer is, for any young person who is 13 or even younger, if you are mature enough to read this book, start making life's important decisions.

Now that you have gotten a hold of this book, read it, study the Word (the Bible), and become a good and faithful child of God. Living our life and walking with God is a wonderful and rewarding experience. After all, we are here on this planet to do what He wants us to do. Knowing the will of God for our lives and following the leading of the Holy Spirit is exciting.

Furthermore, knowing His will can avoid lot of unnecessary heartaches and troubles. That doesn't mean becoming a Christian means no more problems. There will be trials, but knowing that God is there for us and fighting the battles for us is priceless. You have to be there to experience the joy. I strongly believe that, to be called a child of God is the highest honour.

I have two daughters and I am so thankful to God that they both serve the Lord. When they left home for university I was sad, but I had such peace that God the Father was taking care of them both, and *all* their needs. I just dedicated them to the Lord when they left home and I dedicated them to the Lord EVERY SINGLE DAY in my prayers. I still do that. It was easy only because I knew God is my father and their father too. He is a father to the fatherless (see Psalms 68:5a). Now, one of my daughters is married, and she is married to someone from the Catholic background. But he knew right from the start that he had to accept Jesus as his Lord and Saviour before the friendship could go forward any further. Since I don't have a husband, I had the 'assignment' to break it to him when he, both my daughters and I met for lunch for the first time. I talked to him very politely. Getting the message across was the purpose. He took it very well. He always attended the church with us and we never pressured him. But we were all praying for his salvation and it happened. Then, only after then, they got married.

That said, my prayer is that every young person reading this book will follow through, and have a very happy, successful Christian life. There will be challenges, but hang in there and God will come through for you every time. You might need to fast and pray sometimes or ask for the prayers of others. Don't just run to anybody and everybody when you have issues. You go to God first and then see where He is leading you. Turn to a praying friend for their support in prayer. For married people; I always say if you have a praying spouse it is heaven on earth. The support of the spouse is so important in each other's life. You can pray together. Prayer is such a powerful tool because it gives us access to the Almighty God through Jesus Christ. If you are a young person, as you get a little older you need to know the basic steps involved in doing what God wants you to do about your future, higher education (university, college etc.), choosing a career, choosing your spouse, buying a home etc. After reading this book you will find out how important it is to hear the voice of God and how to act on it. If you're not sure you should pray for the guidance of the Holy Spirit and seek counsel from a mentor or someone with whom you have the oneness of spirit.

It is very important where we go for counseling. First, not all counsel is from God. So you need to discern the spirit, which means you have to make sure this person is working with God and not with the enemy. When in doubt stick with somebody you know that is of God. You definitely need to spend time alone in prayer, just you and the Lord. While asking Him for guidance, you need to stop and listen to what God is telling you. Later on in this book, I'll be talking about prayer to help you learn how to pray effectively.

SWEET SURENDER

This is my story how I totally surrendered to
God, the one who created me and sent me here
to serve His plan and purpose. I didn't find that
out until after I went through my divorce. Okay,
you might ask, "Isn't it wrong for a Christian
to get a divorce?" But mine was not a God
approved marriage to start off with, so it didn't
survive. We stayed together for 23 years. It
was very miserable, not a single, I mean not a
single day with peace. I had no idea what was
wrong. I blamed it on him he blamed it on me.
So it boggled my mind. I prayed for him "please
Lord change him "and nothing happened then
I started praying for me, change me Lord. I just
wanted my marriage to work. After I learned
that, I was not the only woman in this world
who wanted a husband, a nice home and the
security of all that, I started fasting and praying.
I thought "I am not giving up. Is the grass really
greener on the other side of the fence or does it
just look green from here?" I was trying to talk
myself into staying in the marriage. So, it went
on for a few years and when I became pregnant

with my first daughter, I thought things would change when the baby came along. Nothing changed, and two years later, my second child was born. At that point things started to get even worse. From then on it was downhill. I kept asking the Lord show me what I did wrong. Why are you punishing me like this? Growing up I was a very obedient child to my parents. I wasn't perfect, but I was a good Christian girl, never hurt anyone, never deceived anyone. I prayed, read my bible twice daily. I continued my habit of prayer and bible reading even after I got married.

To top it off, even though I was still in this miserable marriage, I was a "good Christian girl" and I wasn't even getting a divorce. I kept reminding myself that I could not get a divorce. It says in Malachi 2:16 that Jehovah hates divorce. So I said, "I have to stay in this marriage". I kept telling God, as if He doesn't know, "Lord I'm doing all these just to please you, not because I really want to, so why aren't you giving me peace and happiness?" (Psalms 139:1-4 clearly says we cannot hide anything from God . . . He knows even our inner most thoughts . . .)

My prayers were getting stronger and stronger and I never missed a Sunday church service. Even when we travelled to visit our family and

friends, I made sure we attended a church. I had
to make sure I did everything pleasing to God.
In the meantime, the marriage was suffering
and there was no peace in the family. The only
time we enjoyed peace was when others were
in our house or when we visited others. In other
words when we were alone there was always
disharmony. He was angry all the time. He was
very, very unhappy and negative. It was starting
to affect the children. Since my side of the family
had been around, the children didn't miss out on
the love of family. But that should be secondary.
Children need the love of their parents first.
EVERY CHILD DESERVES A HAPPY HOME! A
LOVING FATHER AND A LOVING MOTHER! The
parents owe it to them. Of course, the mother's
love is unconditional. But I never had the
support of my husband in that area, since he
didn't want any children.

When we get out of God's will, we won't have
any peace. It may look like we have everything. It
did in our case. Everything looked good on the
outside: we lived in a nice 4 bedroom house, had
a good business, the children went to a private
school etc, but there was no peace. I was even
suicidal. Twice I made plans to kill myself and
the children by turning the engine of my car
on in the garage with the door closed. I made

plans the night before I went to bed but in the morning I chickened out . . . I couldn't do it. I know that evil thought was not from God, but I did not know what else to do or where to turn to.

After my separation, I did some research on physical abuse and found out that most women are like me. They won't talk about it to anyone because it is embarrassing. Eventually, we learn things the hard way or God teaches us things, so we can be where He wants us to be.

So, after 23 years of marriage I decided to leave *my husband*. I had many green lights from the Lord to move out or separate myself permanently from him. But I kept reminding myself scripture says "God hates divorce". So I stayed married until the Lord assured me it's okay to get out of this union. One night I had a dream that the man I was married to was hitting me and I woke up sobbing. I looked over to see him lying beside me sleeping. I felt much better; at least this time no one's hitting me; it was not real—it was just a dream. So I decided to go back to sleep. Just as I put my head on the pillow, falling asleep, I woke up hearing a voice telling me, "he hurt you too much. I want you to come out of there. "Wow! Who's there? I sat up in my bed and looked out towards the door to see who was standing there. The voice was so clear and so near that I wanted to know who was talking to me. I must say it was a man's voice. The beautiful part was I wasn't scared at all but wondered who it was. I knew for a fact that I heard a real voice and it was not my imagination. The only man in the house was in deep sleep, so it had to come from another source.

Even though, at that point I didn't know much about the audible voice of God, inside of me I felt happy knowing that *for the first time ever* someone's agreeing with me and trying to help me. That was very comforting. But I didn't even think it was anything supernatural. I kept thinking about it, saying, "that was weird, what was it?" etc. It was not leaving my mind. In my world, God only talked to important godly people. I was just an ordinary woman working hard, running a business, trying to make my marriage work, raise the kids in the best possible way I could. Besides, I was still trying to make things work at least for me and the children. I had to do the best I could to give them a good future. Of course, I knew the bible talks about it in the book of 1 Samuel chapter 3. We read about Samuel as a young boy hearing the audible voice of God when God called him by his name "Samuel, Samuel" to tell him to give a message to Eli. But for me, that was the last thing on my mind. Not because I didn't want to hear God calling me and talking to me, but to tell you the truth, until I got the interpretation of that event I didn't even think it happened in this day and age. Nevertheless, that voice in the supernatural gave me the strength to go tell the man I was married to that we should consider separation . . . That was a miracle!

Taking the first step was the hardest. I still couldn't tell him it was over. A husband, two children, a false security, etc. But like I said, the voice from the Lord gave me the strength. So, the next day I told him, "I'm going to sleep in the spare bedroom, you can sleep in the bedroom." The first night was the hardest, I wanted to go back to my familiar bed. But something inside of me kept saying "NO". In the days that followed, the voice I heard kept coming back to my mind. It just wouldn't leave. Finally one day the Holy Spirit led me to 2 Corinthians 6: 17 & 18."Leave them, separate yourselves from them, don't touch their filthy things, and I will welcome you and be a father to you and you will be my children." Wow! That is what it was. It made so much sense to me.

After that, we continued to live in the same house but separate rooms for a few more

months until we decided to move out and go
our separate ways. We had to wait until we broke
it to his family and my family. At that point I
phoned my older brother, living a few thousand
miles away from us, and told him about the
decision to "separate" and eventually divorce.
He was very sad to hear about it, but he also
told me that he had a dream few days before.
In the dream he saw my house, and a man in
a long white gown with a fluffy animal on His
shoulder came in to the house and took me and
my girls with Him. When he told me about the
dream I knew exactly what it meant and to this
day my brother doesn't remember that dream.
Saddened by the "divorce news", he told me,
"please don't do anything yet. I want to come
and see you both and talk to you both in person.
Maybe I can help you reconcile." My answer was
kind of uncertain, but I said "Yes." We cannot fool
God. When God closes a door nobody can open
it. I made my decision:

1. I'd better not disobey God

2. Nobody or nothing will make me change
    the vow I made to God in private "my
    marriage is over and I will follow you
    and you alone Lord, because there is no
    one above you."

SECOND CHANCE

God is a God of second chances. The last 2 years of my marriage, I didn't realize I was doing something wrong when I stopped going to church and stopped having prayer at home, all to please the man I was married to. I was just listening to family and some close friends that said I should love him and keep him happy by doing things to please him. They said God only comes after your husband. They convinced me that if I couldn't please him I couldn't love God. ALWAYS REMEMBER SATAN HIDES BEHIND FAMILIAR FACES.

Again I was being told, DIVORCE IS WRONG. I wrestled with that thought for a long time until I got confirmations over and over and over and over again because in certain situations God allows divorce. After I got the explanation I was *waiting* for, *I was sure* I got the **green light** from God to get out of that marriage. I lost my home, which God promised me when we had moved into the house that He would help me pay the mortgage off in 5 years. The year after we moved into the house, God blessed me with a business which I always wanted, and the business really flourished for a while. After 7 years I had to leave that too. Isaiah 1:19 says if we are obedient, we will eat the fruit of the land . . . . but to stop serving God is BIG HUGE disobedience.

The movers came and moved our furniture into storage, the house was empty now. As I was standing in my kitchen with tears rolling down my face, I said, "Lord, you told me you'll help me pay off the mortgage in 5 years". I was planning on putting a swimming pool in the back yard and other renovations. When I moved in that house I said, "this is it; I don't want to move again until the children are grown and married" and so on. So I asked God, "What happened? Why are we leaving?" I got an answer right away. I heard a faint buzzing like a bee right into my ear. I heard these words "sometimes I change my mind". LESSON LEARNED; GOD'S PROMISES ARE CONDITIONAL!! They are conditional upon obeying God! Plain and Simple!

So here we are, moving into an apt since we made arrangements to move out of the house, the 4 of us. My brother came and tried to talk to us but *who can undo what God has done?* We don't put a question mark where the Lord has put a period. The man I was married to gave my brother some negative answers. My brother said to me "it looks like you have done the right thing." Since we were spiritually mismatched, we just couldn't be married to each other; 2 Corinthians 6:14 & 15 clearly talks about this. Verse 14a says "Don't be teamed with those who do not love the Lord." You might ask, "what about the believer man or woman living with an unbeliever spouse?" The Apostle Paul says if the spouse doesn't want to leave the wife or husband, let them stay together. Trust me, I asked the Lord all these questions. The answer every time was OBEY GOD AND LEAVE THE CONSEQUENCES TO GOD. Who am I to argue with God? I learned that the hard way. Because of the physical abuse, divorce was allowed. He always had so much anger inside of him. He hated being married. God doesn't like to see His children getting hurt.

HOW DO WE KNOW IT IS GOD TALKING TO US?

1. *God speaks to us through dreams.* In the book of Genesis chapter 41, we read Pharaoh had a dream and Joseph was called to interpret that dream. Joseph did such a good job he even got promoted in the palace.

2. *God can speak to us through a song.* We will feel a stirring in our spirit listening to a song. Or a sense of peace. Then we know its God.

3. *God can talk to us through a Bible verse.* We might have read the same verse before but at that point of our need God is meeting us by speaking through that Bible verse. It will jump out and bring comfort and peace or the answer to our question. Then we know it is God.

4. *When we pray or worship God.* In these times we get ideas in our mind probably

about a future career or for higher education. That's God planting ideas in us, saying "this what I want for you, my child." Even after we receive a promise we need to pray for the fulfillment of that promise. Ask the spirit of God to guide you on that.

5. *Somebody prophesying over you about your future.* I guess on that one you will know it is God speaking through a servant, as long as you know he or she is truly sent by God, and speaking under the anointing of God. From my experience it is ALWAYS a confirmation of something that was already on my mind. In this case perhaps you had a thought in your mind for a while and kept it on the back burner, so to speak, or you might have brushed it off, and it just got resurrected by that prophecy.

6. *God can talk to us through a sermon.* You could be sitting with 2,000 or 20,000 other people in an auditorium. A meeting you went into with a special burden or a need and you got an answer. There were others in the same room with other needs and a few of

them got their answers also from the same sermon. That's how the Holy Spirit works in people's lives; He will interpret the same message or the same sermon according to the individual situation. As you start growing in the Lord, you'll also find that you might get the same bible verse that you got when you were looking for a word from God that gave you comfort or the answer you needed 5 years ago, in a totally different situation. Now again, the exact same verse is being translated for your need this time.

7. *The small, quiet voice.* When God told me (you get these thoughts and ideas) to take water baptism I said, "Lord I was baptized as a baby, why do I have to do it again? After all it's just an outward thing . . . . Isn't it a clean heart that matters to you?" Raised in one of the main line churches, I couldn't even lift my hands in church to praise God when I started going to the evangelical church, let alone go in front of the whole church to the baptismal tank and get immersed in the water. Besides, I'm the kind of person who wants to know why it is necessary. A little explanation. Not

that I am stubborn or anything. It is no exaggeration, at least it felt that way, everywhere I turned, all the messages on the radio while driving to places or even on television sometimes, were about adult baptism. In other words God convinced me that I must do it. So I called the church office and arranged to take baptism with the next group. Trust me, when the time came I was so ready, I was weeping all the way up to the baptismal tank because of the power of the anointing of God on me, and it was so rewarding. I'd like to add another line about water baptism while we are talking about it: Water baptism is the 2nd step in our salvation program.

HOW DO I KNOW WHAT IS GOD'S WILL FOR MY LIFE?

I'm going to give you 4 main ways to know the will of God.

1. *Word of God.* Whatever you think you heard from God has to line up with God's word. This means you have to make sure that particular situation is allowed in the Bible not against the teaching in the Bible.

2. *Something God has brought to you.* For example: You're looking for a mate. May be you're not really looking, but praying, and suddenly God through someone else will introduce you to a potential mate. Or by a divine appointment, such as when you are sitting in a coffee shop minding your own business someone comes over to talk to you, or even in any other situation where something you didn't go after was brought to you. Yeah, you could say it "dropped in my lap"

sort of thing. Beware! Not everything "dropped in your lap" is from God. You have to find that out by praying for confirmations or more signs.

3. *Something that stands the test of time*. Something persistent, it won't go away, keeps coming back to your mind.

4. *Someone prophesying over you.* The message in most cases should be something you are already thinking about or already had on your mind for a while. Someone will come with a message from God to confirm your thoughts. So now you can move forward with that. Remember, continue to seek God on that in prayer. If we stop praying God cannot move in our life.

Okay, whatever you experience, you still have to pray about it. Pray that God will guide you and lead you to the next step and so on. When God gives a promise, that is God's way of telling us "I have a plan and purpose for you!" Then we get all excited and think it's going to happen the next day, or the next week or, at longest, next month. I'm not saying all God's promises are late in coming to pass. On some things, we get

an answer in a week. I find that earlier on in my
walk with God I got answers pretty quickly, and
often. Once you get to know God and become
more and more familiar with Him and His ways,
you can learn to be patient when some things
take a little longer to come to pass. Our faith is
being strengthened and we can help others in
the same situation.

God wants to take us from *"Glory to Glory"*. He
doesn't want us to stay in one place. He wants us
to grow. Whatever the situation you are in, once
you know it is God's will, seek Him earnestly.!
God will take us through different paths to mold
our character. That is the idea. Once we accept
Jesus as our Lord and Saviour the *journey* starts.
We have to become more and more like Jesus.
I love the WWJD (what would Jesus do) slogan.
Saying it is easy. Practicing it is the hardest. Like
everything else, the old saying "easier said than
done" works here. It's not always the way we
think God wants it. It's not about us. It's all about
God. About Jesus. We are the vessels God uses.
That is why *humility* is a good character trait for
a believer. Look at Jeremiah 29: 11-13. God is
saying "For I know the plans I have for you. They
are plans for good and not for evil, to give you a
future and a hope. In those days when you pray I
will listen. You will find me when you seek me, IF

you look for me earnestly." So, getting a promise is good news but we have work to do to achieve it. Like I said earlier, a promise from God means He is on our side in this situation so we can move forward knowing full well God will help us, prosper us, and He will come through for us.

YOUR CALLING AND YOUR GIFTING

Our calling and our gifting may not be the same. We see in the book of Exodus chapter 3, God is calling Moses. Continue reading chapter 4, see verses 10, 11& 12. God calls the unqualified and He qualifies them. Our job is to just obey. Here God is telling Moses, "I already know about your stuttering. I'm the one who created you. I have a plan and purpose for creating you. It's time for you to go and fulfill what your destiny is here on this earth." Your calling and your gifting can be the same. For example, maybe you can sing very well, you like to sing, you want to sing and you get these promptings from the Holy Spirit that you should be singing in public before a crowd. At that point you have a desire in your heart to sing in public. Then you should start praying that God will open doors. He will put the right people (contacts) in your path. That is what I call 'God planting desires in us'. Please read 1 Corinthians 12:8-11. This passage is talking about our spiritual gifts. See if you have any of these gifts. See also Romans 12:6-9.

Do you want to know how you can find out what your GIFTING is? When I was searching for my gifts, this is what the Holy Spirit brought to me. This is from a few years back and I still remember it. It makes so much sense. Here you go.

1. Something you are very good at.

2. Something you really enjoy doing.

3. Something other people compliment you on.

Now, let's talk about your CALLING. You may not always see the burning bush and hear the audible voice of God like Moses did (Exodus 3:2). We all have a special way of receiving messages from God. For example, for me, 2 times I heard the audible voice of God. Both times there was a dream along with that. I had the dream first and then the voice. Both the events happened within 2 years of each other. When it happened the second time, I knew right away it was God. The second dream and voice was about a future event or God promising me something for my future. Since I had a previous experience, as soon as I woke up from my sleep I understood what had just happened, and I was so excited about the promise and the presence of God in my life. I still remember when I woke up I was still talking, asking God a question. I asked Him "really? For me?" The second one happened 15 years ago. God talks to me through other sources too.

Your calling, in simple English, is your assignment on this earth. We are here on this earth to do what God has sent us to do. This is not our eternal home; we are just passing through here. While we are here fulfilling His plan and purpose for our life, we go to school, study hard to get good marks, get involved in sports and activities, some go to university/college (some may not), we find a job, find a mate, get married, buy a house, have children, and so on and so forth. Some are called to be doctors, some are called to be lawyers, Police men, teachers, pastors, the CEO of a corporation, some have administrative abilities and are called to be in charge of the work of others. The Bible says if God has given us money, be generous in helping others in need. When you are a believer you dedicate your life to the Lord.

Especially, when you are young, even before you reach 12 or 13 you should ask the Lord what He wants you to be. If God wants you to be a doctor and you are even afraid of needles, you wonder how that's going to happen. Wait a minute, yes!

God can change you, if that is what God created you to be and sent to this earth for.

Remember we talked about Moses earlier? When God called him to deliver God's people from the oppression of Pharaoh in Egypt, Moses said "I'm not the right person for this job." Starting in Exodus chapter 3 going to chapter 4, Moses is still arguing with God that he cannot do this job. Finally, pleading with God, he says in verse 10 "O Lord, I'm not a good speaker. I never have been, and I'm not now, even AFTER YOU HAVE SPOKEN TO ME, for I have a speech impediment." Watch what God's answer in verse 11 is: "Who makes mouths? Isn't it I, the Lord? Who makes a man so that he can speak or not speak, see or not see, hear or not hear?" (Please look at verse 12 very carefully) They are having a conversation like two people are talking to each other sitting in a coffee shop. God Himself is promising this. "Now go ahead and do as I tell you, for I will help you to speak well, and I will tell you what to say." COME ON! If God and I ever have a face to face conversation like this, then I don't need any more confirmation, I don't need any more signs. Even if I'm afraid of needles and God says He wants me to be a doctor, I'll say, "YES LORD, send me, I'll go!" My point is, if God is the one giving you the assignment and you're sure of it, no matter who says what against it, or what your feelings are on it, you can count on God to equip you! REMEMBER: He calls the unqualified and qualifies them.

Prayer life is very important for a Christian. Prayer is communicating with God. Don't ever try to get out of God's will. If you say "no" to God, that is disobedience on your part. Delaying in doing what God tells us to do is also disobedience. Well, life must go on, so God will send somebody else in your place. Just because you said "no" to a task God gave you, it doesn't mean God will cancel the project. If you surrender your life totally to God, He will help you. It sure is a partnership. John 15:5 says "Yes, I am the Vine and you are the branches. Whoever lives in me and I in him shall produce a large crop of fruit. For apart from me you can do nothing."

FAITH

I'd like to talk a little bit about FAITH. Hebrews 11:1 says "Faith is the confident assurance that something we want is going to happen. It is the certainty that what we hope for is waiting for us, even though we cannot see it up ahead in the natural. "Verse 6 says, "you can never please God without faith, without depending on Him. Anyone who wants to come to God must believe that there is a God and that He rewards those who sincerely look for Him."

We say, by faith we received Jesus Christ as our Lord and Saviour. But the faith I'm talking about is a gift from God as mentioned in 1 Corinthians 12:9. This is a special, supernatural gift, given to us by God. Let's take the example of Father Abraham. We read in Genesis chapter 12 starting at verse 1, about how God called Abraham to leave the familiar country and go wherever God was leading him. I'm VERY MUCH encouraged by what Abraham did. We should all be. He had no road map, no GPS, no directions at all, yet he obeyed what God told him to do. Verse 2 says,

"If you do what I just told you to do I will cause you to become the father of a great nation. I will bless you and make your name famous and you will be a blessing to many others". When it's not clear where we are going, obey God. The Bible says Abraham was 75 years old. How old? 75 years old. Well, many events took place in 24 years, including the birth of Ishmael. God said He will bless Ishmael also (see ch.17: 20). Now Abraham is 99 years old when God appeared to him (see Genesis 17: 21), and said "I'll establish a covenant with Isaac" (we read in verse 19 God says, "Sarah shall have a child next year about this time and they should call him Isaac") whom Sarah will bear to you. Try to remember these two verses; we'll come back to it after. So Isaac was born a year later, when Abraham was 100 years old, and Sarah was 90 years old.

FAITH AND OBEDIENCE GO HAND IN HAND.

Later on God tested Abraham's faith and obedience by telling him to sacrifice his son Isaac. Abraham obeyed God, and didn't ask any questions. Now, see in Genesis chapter 22:5 (IS THIS FAITH OR WHAT?) Abraham is telling his two servants "you young men wait here, Isaac and I will go over there and worship and . . ." (see these are Abraham 's words) "The **lad and**

I will be back." Abraham knew in his heart that somehow he's taking Isaac back home with him (either God will say it's ok don't sacrifice the boy, or there will be an animal ready, or even after Isaac was sacrificed and died God will bring him back to life). Whatever thoughts were going on in Abraham's mind the highlight here is his *faith* based on God's promise in Genesis chapter 17:19 & 21. He was holding on to those words God PROMISED him, that through Isaac (son of Sarah) He would bless the nations. So Isaac had to be around to fulfill that promise. In the same way, when God gives us a promise, if there is any testing period, we need to persevere because God is testing our faith and teaching us to be stronger; He is preparing us for bigger things. Don't give up or give in. Why am I talking so much about faith? The bible says it is impossible to please God without faith (Hebrews 11:6). Our part is obedience without compromise. In Mark 9:23 Jesus says **"anything is possible if you have faith".**

I just want to use one more example of GREAT FAITH: Noah. Please read Genesis chapters 6 & 7 to understand the story. God told Noah that there is going to be a flood to destroy the earth and that he should build an ark to save himself, his wife, his three sons and their wives, the birds and animals. These were God's instructions for Noah. The bible says in Hebrews 11:7, when Noah heard God's warning about the future, he believed God even though there was then no sign of flood. And he built the ark. So the key is **Trust and Obey!**

One day I heard God saying to me that I should go to bible college. I said "Lord how do I do that? You know I need to put the girls through university and I don't see it happening . . ." Then "out of the blue" (we don't have out of the blue experiences or coincidences, it's always the Holy Spirit) my church started a one year training program for lay people wanting to go into ministry and leadership roles in the church. (If you have the pre-requisite, you're accepted for the course, which I had.) For the 1st year I wasn't sure if that was for me. Sure enough though, the Holy Spirit led me (actually, pressured me) to take it the next year and I successfully completed it.

After completing the course, the church placed me as a facilitator for the support group for divorced people. Then I was asked to lead the Singles Ministry and to do the Bible study for singles. Both I did for 7 years. I'm still doing a Bible study for a small group. I'm also currently working on another project the Lord gave me.

OBEDIENCE IS BETTER THAN SACRIFICE PART 1 (1 SAMUEL 15:22)

God reminded me of the time He told me to go into a ministry which served the university students and I went to a weekend conference in a nearby city. After attending the conference back then, I didn't think it was for me. I was very excited to go to the conference but things didn't go the way I thought they would. I said to myself, "this is not for me. I should look into something else and move on with my life". I still remember, it was a fork or a crossroad in my life. I was very anxious to make a decision in regards to choosing my career. What I didn't know at that time was that God really wanted me to pursue working with university students He directed me to go into, even though it didn't look like it was for me.

I never thought God would use someone like me, meaning, just a lay person, a female in a male dominated society. The truth of the matter is, when Jesus came to set the captives free He liberated the women too. According to Matthew 28:10 on Sunday morning after He was raised from the dead Jesus asked the women to "go tell my brothers to leave at once for Galilee to meet me there." Jesus gave so much importance to the women. They hung out with Him or I should say He hung out with them. Also, in the book of Joel chapter 2 vs 28 God says" I will pour out My spirit on all flesh; your sons and *daughters* shall prophesy". That is what is expected of every believer. Salvation is not for us to keep, but to share with others, ie. family, friends, neighbours, co-workers, people we meet on the airplane, in the market place, etc. We cannot just go talk to everyone unless we are prompted by the Holy Spirit. Every morning before we leave home we can pray "Lord, whomever you want me to talk to today, or however you want me to reach to someone, I pray that you'll put them in my path, and give me the boldness to share the Good news with them".

An act of kindness in the name of the Lord is something we can do. I remember, recently sitting in a coffee shop having my coffee and reading the newspaper a man came over to me and said, "Hi . . . please don't be grumpy, I'm homeless, if you can give me some money . . ."

I looked at him and said "I don't have a lot on
me but I'll give you something, and I want you
to know where I go when I need something." He
stood waiting to hear what I had to say. I said,
"I just ask Jesus . . . Have you heard of Jesus?"
He said, "yes." I said,"So all you need to do is
just ask him. He will definitely help you" He said,
"okay", took the money, and left. Something
similar happened a month before that. It was a
bright sunny day, in a busy parking lot, and as
I was getting out of my car to go into a store a
man approached me. I noticed he had talked to
another woman before he came to me. He said
he was homeless and needed some money. I
ignored him and walked into the store. When
I came out of the store I saw him still in the
parking lot going to different people, nobody
even looked at him. I got into my car drove over
to where he was and said, "here is some money
for you, but I want you to know when I need
something I go to Jesus and He helps me every
time." I asked him if he heard of Jesus, and he
said "yes". I said, "well you go talk to Him, He will
help you". The man said, "Thank you. God Bless"
and I drove off.

I'm not saying every single believer will talk to
one or more people every single day. We can ask
ourselves the question "am I ready and willing

to do this for the Lord?" I know some people are so good at street evangelism. Okay, if you're not comfortable with that, then ask the Lord "where can I serve you?" That is a must for every believer!!!! You will be amazed what doors God will open for you.

OBEDIENCE IS BETTER THAN SACRIFICE PART 2

Previously, I talked about God calling me to go into ministry but I didn't even give it a second thought when I decided to go into another profession. I had already completed my undergraduate, and got a bachelor's degree in Economics. I started my Master's and had a couple other ideas for furthering my education. Neither of them worked out. God wanted me to go into ministry. I never had learned from anywhere how to discern God's voice. It was all new to me and I didn't even know it was God talking to me. I thought it was just a thought in my flesh and brushed it off. In other words, I didn't understand the calling I had on my life at that point. Of course, I prayed for things after I decided to do something, but I was never taught to seek God first to see if it is God's will. That was my main line church upbringing. I prayed in the morning, said grace before every meal, prayed before I went to bed. Those are all the basic prayers. I was baptized as a baby and I had my confirmation ceremony when I was 13 years old. But because I didn't really have the personal relationship with Jesus, there was confusion sometimes that went with the counsel of others mainly people who were older than me; the "more experienced people". Usually, after the decision had been made I would pray for it and pray over it. I always liked praying, I enjoyed singing, and I naturally took leadership roles. I was and am a leader, hardly a follower. Except to Jesus. I don't think I'm arrogant by any means, in fact I think I am more on the humble side because I'm very uncomfortable if I act bossy and arrogant. I know that is the GRACE of God on my life, I know that for a fact! For that reason I do not enjoy being with arrogant people either, even to this day. In general, I feel bad for them for being ignorant, because in my opinion they lack godly wisdom. I always pray especially after I've been placed on leadership roles "Lord make me humble like Moses". The Bible says in the book of Numbers chapter 12: 3 Moses was the humblest man on earth. I believe if you're an approachable person you will attract more people.

In my younger days I didn't know much about the prompting of the Holy Spirit. I prayed for my needs, my school and my family. I just did pretty much everything my parents taught me. I was involved in youth ministry, taught Sunday school, sang in the church choir etc. What I'm saying is, even though I was involved in church activities, those are all more of an organizational ministry rather than something of an individual ministry; something of my own. When I look at it now I guess I can say I did things for God in general. Others asked me to be there and I said yes.

I was out of God's will when I decided not to take up the Holy Spirit's leading to go into the ministry working with University students. Because of my sin (disobedience) my spiritual eyes and my spiritual ears were closed. I couldn't see or hear God. So how could I make a decision that was good for my future? The Israelites were in the wilderness for 40 years, even though they started the journey with the plan to walk over to the promised land in just 11 days (Deuteronomy 1: 2 & 3)

Disobedience is a barrier to knowing God's will. We often want to do what we think is a better plan. Once we realize He knows what is best and He has the best in store for us, we will learn to submit and surrender. Another thing about being in God's will is that you will feel total peace. No matter how much money we have or how many close friends and loving family we have, nothing will ever bring us peace if we are out of the will of God. That is actually one way of knowing if we are in God's will. PEACE. Isaiah 26:3 says "you will keep him in perfect peace whose mind is stayed on you. Because he trusts in you"

Climbing the ladder of success won't give the peace we're looking for. It feels like something is not right or like we can't ever have the total happiness we are looking for. On the other hand, even if we don't have much material wealth, if we are in God's will, we're always happy. ***That' s the Joy of the Lord!*** I know this because I have experienced it. I've been on both sides of the fence, so to speak. What I have now in the Lord I wouldn't trade it for anything or anybody. Once we start to obey God, the Holy Spirit will guide us and lead us. We will become sensitive to the leading of the Holy Spirit because we can see and hear now.

When I was around 12-13 yrs old I often talked about becoming a lawyer. My grandmother always said "well, that is not a good profession for a Christian, since lawyers have to lie in the court for their clients", and so on. (I am not making a statement here. I'm just saying what my grandmother told me. I know some lawyers who attend my church who are good people.)

At that point I had to pick another profession, so I "chose" to get rich by becoming a business woman.

When I was 26, I bought my first business, a money making business. It was a gold mine. I kept thinking that God dropped this in my lap. God made it possible for me to buy the business and prosper. All the things I learned from it have been very useful. God knew I needed the knowledge and experience for later in my life. I owned that business for 3 years and sold it when my daughter turned 1, so that I could raise her myself, since I didn't believe in babysitters or even a nanny. A year later, I decided to have another child. In a few months I gave birth to my 2nd child. Through all these events, I thought I was really in the will of God, and I did my best to please God in everything I did. I started fasting and praying continuously for my marriage because I didn't want a divorce

A few years passed by, my family life was getting worse and it was affecting the children indirectly. They were suffering emotionally. There was always disharmony, no peace, no unity. The kids watched television quite a bit. I, in my lack of knowledge, or should I say lack of wisdom, allowed it. Things were still going downhill. I

Salee Davids

fasted and prayed more and more. I still stayed in the marriage. But obeying God is much better than keep on praying against God's will. Things are not getting any better only worse. I was suicidal and made plans to kill myself and the kids twice. Both times when the time came I just couldn't do it. GOD SPARED MY LIFE TO FULFILL HIS PLAN AND PURPOSE. PRAISE THE LORD!

SALVATION

I just want to talk a little bit about getting saved. To me there are 3 steps involved in salvation.

1. We accept Jesus as the Lord and Saviour by somebody praying with us in person or on television. Or maybe you just decided to do it in your bedroom or apartment prompted by the Holy Spirit. Just you and the Lord. So they led you to Jesus, so to speak. We generally refer to it as "getting saved". Right at that moment the Holy Spirit starts living in us.

2. Water baptism is the outward expression of what just took place in us. We are declaring that we died to the flesh by immersing in the water (die to our sins) and rise with Christ as a new person.

3. If you are an evangelical Christian there is something called "the baptism of the Holy Spirit". That is what is generally known as speaking in tongues because

when you start speaking in tongues (other languages unknown to you, sometimes unknown on earth), that means you got the Holy Spirit infilling. Speaking in tongues is the (outside) sign. But you still need to practice it to get better at it, or if you don't use it you could even lose it. I'm not saying you need the infilling of the Holy Spirit to go to heaven, but it sure is a bonus for your Christian life here on this earth. We believe when we get the infilling or the baptism of the Holy Spirit we start to speak in tongues, according to Acts chapter 2:4. There are 2 primary uses for this gift.

A. To pray in the spirit, meaning praying in an unknown language. We believe it is only understood by God (father, son & Holy Spirit) and the enemy won't interfere. Especially when you're praying about impossible situations it will come in really handy.

B. If you are an English speaking person you start speaking in a foreign language, that message is for someone in your group who only speaks that particular language and they don't understand English. You never went to school to learn that particular language but God just gave you the anointing for that occasion to reach out to the person or simply putting it, God's spirit just spoke through you.

THE *SPIRITUAL* BOOT CAMP

I had heard spiritual leaders talking about rising up early in the morning to pray and read the word. But I had always thought that was not for me since I was not a morning person. When I was in high school and university I stayed up late, as late as 2am some days to study. The earliest I got up was 6:30am. But then God started talking to me about getting up early in the morning to spend time with Him. He made it very clear to me that I needed to get up at 4am everyday to do my devotions. When I was so sure that I needed to do this, I wasn't sad or angry or unsure or any of those negative states of mind. Instead I was so excited and looking forward to this meeting with the Holy Spirit every morning. I even had a separate alarm clock just for this. Some mornings I was already awake before the alarm went off. It was something I was so looking forward to doing first thing in the morning. In fact, I would get excited about the meeting with the Lord in the morning, even when I went to bed the previous night. So, that means I started everyday with the Lord.

Not only did I start the day with the Lord, because I spent about an hour or more every morning, when I went into the world to do my earthly duties I always had the Holy Spirit guiding me and directing me. Literally my steps were ordered by the Lord. You may ask what I mean by this statement. Well, sometimes things make too much sense. Sometimes, it's hard for me to understand how I did it. I had no plan to do whatever it may be, but it was the Holy Spirit moving my hands and my feet and my mouth to speak etc. Do you want to know the most beautiful part for me? ***I always had total peace***. Something I never had before. Like I mentioned earlier, even when I was climbing the ladder of success, I had no peace. There was something major missing in my life. Lots of toiling but very few results, or not really getting where I wanted to go. Now I know that's God's way of telling us "you are out of my will", and His favour is not on our life.

Right after my separation I started attending a Pentecostal church with my two daughters. They previously had attended the Christian School run by the same church. Every time I passed by some power was pulling me towards this church like a magnet. When I was in my marriage I tried to go to this church but, after a short time the man

I was married to said to me if I continued to go to this church I cannot come home. One Sunday evening as usual, I got ready and grabbed my keys and started towards the front door. He came over and said, "where are you going?" I said, "to church". He said, "if you go to that church, don't come back here," and he pushed me out and locked the door. I stood in the patio and started talking to God. I said "Lord you're the one who showed me this church, told me to fast Sunday nights, and attend the evening service at the church. How can I do this if there's no harmony in my home?. You need to talk to him." I stood there for about 15 min and came back in. That was the end of my church going until after my separation.

After we got separated, the very next Sunday I started going to this church again in the mornings and in the evenings. The Holy Spirit laid on my heart to fast in the mornings and evenings just to honour God. He said to keep the Sabbath holy (Exodus 20:8) which I started to do, and I usually have a good lunch on Sundays.

Then God told me about taking water baptism which I mentioned earlier. Coming from a main line background I said, "Lord you know my parents baptized me as baby. What difference does it make when it is only an outward thing anyway?" Oh yeah! Oh yeah! For a few months everywhere I turned I heard about adult baptism and I was convinced it was necessary. Finally I surrendered and called the church, and joined the next group of people taking water baptism. It had only been 7 months since my separation, and I was making great progress in my walk with the Lord. I also started attending the mid-week bible study at the church. I was running a business and God told me to get rid of it. I tried to sell it but God told me to just close it down and come follow Him. After that I was sent into the corporate world to work, making just enough money to pay my rent, car payment, insurance, food etc. I wanted to take other courses and apply for promotions inside the company but God clearly said, "don't climb the corporate ladder, this money is just for your survival while you get to know me more and more". The Lord directed me to go where I was supposed to be going, since I missed a few steps when I got married instead of going into ministry. I had no more material possessions. I lost my house, I lost my business, but I had peace. It was a new beginning for me!

I must add when I heard the audible voice of God while I was still in my marriage I was amazed. I was honored and rejoiced that God almighty really spoke to me. I said "God really knows me!" In the days followed I had such hunger and thirst to grow closer and closer to God and it kept growing. It still does.

FASTING AND PRAYING

Fasting and praying is an integral part of a Christian's life. We can fast a Sunday meal without any particular prayer reason, only because it's the Lord's day and we want to honour God. Fasting doesn't always mean starving, especially if you have a medical condition and you can only fast what you are medically allowed. The idea is to sacrifice something. You can have a light breakfast or skip it altogether and just have liquid only.

When you're praying for a special need, you can do the same kind of fast for 7 days, ie. liquid fast just in the mornings, or you can fast all day except for liquid and have a good meal for supper. You can do a three day fast with no meat at all or no bread and no meat. I've done 21 day fasts a few times.

Again, the idea is to sacrifice something you cannot live without. If you are a coffee person, see if you can sacrifice coffee for a number of days. May be it is chocolate that you think you cannot live without. A 40-day fast is another one of the fasts. Fasting without prayer is not effective. The idea is to spend a lot of time in the presence of the Lord in prayer, worship, reading the word etc. Ask the Lord what you should do. Psalms 37:5 says "Commit everything you do to the Lord. Trust Him to help you do it and He will". That is a powerful promise for anything you are praying about. If you believe it, receive it. God is the one telling you to fast so you're just saying, "Yes Lord I want to do it but you tell me which one to pick." Pretty much that's what it is.

Another reason for fasting is cleansing our bodies and teaching ourselves to be more disciplined. God is a God of order and discipline. When there is disorder we know the presence of God is not there. God is like a good parent wanting the best of everything for their children. Except God is above everything and everyone and His love is unconditional. But there will be consequences if we disobey. That's because God wants us to be good children.

Another reason for fasting is cleansing our bodies and teaching ourselves to be more disciplined. God is a God of order and discipline. When there is disorder we know the presence of God is not there. God is like a good parent wanting the best of everything for their children. Except God is above everything and everyone and His love is unconditional. But there will be consequences if we disobey. That's because God wants us to be good children.

THE NUTRITIONAL BOOT CAMP

God wants us to take care of our bodies. We as Christians believe our body is the temple of the Holy Spirit. That means we need to respect our bodies. When I say respect, I mean look after our bodies very well in every possible way. Make sure everything from what goes into our bodies, including the lotion and the cream we apply to our skin on the outside of our bodies to what goes into our mouth and to our stomach is good for us. Whatever we put on our skin can get absorbed into our bodies through the blood vessels, from what I've learned. Where I go to pick up my cream and lotion the sign says our skin is a vital organ in our body. We need to take care of it.

Let's talk about our eating habits first. Cut off all the "junk foods" as much as you can. We know what they are. Usually potato chips, deep fried foods (French fries), rich cakes, cookies, donuts, soft drinks, too much coffee and tea, chocolate bars, sugary items, etc. come under the "junk food" category. I mean, once in a while it should be okay. On special occasions a piece of birthday cake or anniversary cake should be allowed, but the size of it matters. In this day and age, they are promoting organically grown fruits and vegetables so much, we should look into it. Some may say they are expensive, yes more than the regular kind. And some may even say what they brand as 'Organic' is not all that organic. But in my opinion, even if they are not 100% pure (unfortunately) they are less harmful to our bodies than the regular products. Pray over the food you eat every time by asking the Lord to remove everything that is harmful to your body, to sanctify it, and to bless the food to your body. Also, it is a good habit to thank the Lord for the food when you pray.

Did you know gluttony (over eating and drinking) is a sin? What is over eating? It is eating more than what your body needs. WHO DOESN'T LIKE GOOD FOOD? I love good food, but I try to eat small portions. When I was younger I was taught to eat fast because if you eat slowly you cannot eat much because the communication between your stomach and your brain gets mixed up. Your brain thinks you are full and can't eat anymore. I am not a scientist but I've heard that elsewhere too. Now they say eat small portions and if you need, eat more often. I have learned that we should have a meal every 4 hours. Snacks are allowed in between. Again, no junk foods. It can be fruits and vegetables. They say eating fruits fights bad breath also. So it is beneficial in that area also. No need for sugary mints. I hear on popular health shows on TV that the sugar substitutes used in candies and gums are not healthy. It causes diseases. Why knowingly abuse our bodies, which is the temple of the Holy Spirit?

Drinking water is very important in maintaining good health. Drink lots of water, 6-8 glasses of filtered tap water or spring water. Do not freeze your water and juice bottles if they are not for freezer use. Try to drink at least 4 glasses of water in the morning and the balance during the afternoon and early evening.

God is a God of order and discipline. He wants us to do things in an orderly fashion. By eating sensibly we are keeping our bodies clean too. In fact that is the idea. We already know too much salt is bad for our health. So is too much sugar, and too much carbohydrates (bread, rice, potato etc.). I think we can eat pretty much everything God has given us to enjoy if we use our common sense and eliminate all (as much as we can) the chemicals, additives, preservatives etc. If you need vitamins, take them. Ask your doctor what is needed. If you're under stress Vitamin B Complex is recommended. But consult your doctor on that. These are the things I've learned from my experience.

THE PHYSICAL BOOT CAMP

I don't think there is a single person, if you live in the US or Canada, not aware of the importance of working out. So let's talk a little bit about getting some physical exercise. Again, God wants us to make sure we keep our bodies in good shape by exercising on a regular basis. You may ask why? Is it for the appearance of a person? Sure it helps!! But it is more important for your health. If you or any of your loved ones have, for example, diabetes or high blood pressure, you probably heard that they were advised by their doctor or a medical person on the importance of exercise. I'm not saying you should all join a gym if you are not a member already. It is good if you can afford it. Not everybody can afford it. Or you may not have the time to drive there and back, 1 hour for travelling alone. Mind you, it looks like the fitness centres are opening up in every so many blocks, to accommodate more people. Okay, you don't have the extra money for that. I understand that reason. But you can always go for walks in your neighborhood. Pair up with your spouse or a friend. A brisk walk for

20 minutes daily or 30 minutes every other day will be good. Make sure you do it in daylight and also in safe and not secluded areas. That's just common sense but thought I'll add that anyway. If you live in a condo or in an apartment building they usually have exercise rooms there. Please make use of it. However you choose to do it, please CHOOSE!! It is *mandatory* to do physical exercise. We need to keep our heart, lungs, brain and our body muscles in good working condition. Again, it takes discipline and order to keep at it. I believe in keeping our hands and feet looking pretty as well, not just our face. Go get a pedicure and manicure done once a year, and then maintain it on your own to keep your feet and hands look good. Men are not exempt from it, in my opinion. Okay Guys! No dark color nail polish. We are God's chosen ones and called to be peculiar people, but don't want to be that peculiar. ☺

YOUR PRAYER LIFE

Everyone is familiar with the word PRAYER. But most people find no time to pray. Everyone is busy with their work, children, house work, everything else except prayer. I cannot stress enough how important a person's prayer life is, to have a good, healthy, spiritual life, and hence a good relationship with God. In order for us to enjoy the favour of God on our life prayer is MANDATORY. Deuteronomy 8:18a says "Always remember that it is the Lord your God who gives you power to become rich." We read in The New Testament, in the gospels, Jesus spent a lot of time in prayer. Jesus set an example for us. We as Christians are modeling after Jesus. He definitely is our role model. Okay, so what do we do? I'm just going to give you some helpful hints for starting a prayer life and also to pray effectively. It is important that we get answers to our prayers. Below is an acronym you might want to use when you pray.

ACTSI is the Acronym that I have used in the early days of starting my prayer life. I still use it, then go to my stronger prayers. It is just an order of prayer that will help you start your prayer. There are 4 basic steps involved in your daily prayer.

A. Stands for Adoration, saying how mighty is our God. He is wonderful, He is worthy, Hallelujah and worship him.

C. Stands for confession. We need to confess our sins before we can ask for any needs. Because God is Holy, and since we are not, we have to ask Jesus to intervene. So ask for forgiveness of the mistakes you made (sins).

T. Stands for Thanksgiving. Thank Him for all the blessings in your life.

S. Stands for supplication, which is all your needs. Take it all to the Lord.

I. Stands for intercession. That is praying for other people's needs.

The Lord's Prayer is a very basic prayer. It goes like this: "Our Father in heaven, we honor your holy name. We ask that your kingdom will come now. May your will be done here on this earth just as it is in heaven. Give us our food (which means everything we need for our daily living) again today as usual, and forgive us our sins JUST AS WE HAVE FORGIVEN (it is important that we forgive others who offend us) those who have sinned against us. Don't bring us into temptation, but deliver us from the evil one. For Yours is the kingdom, the Power and the Glory, forever and ever. Amen." This is a very simple, basic prayer and it includes everything we need for our daily survival. Here we see a condition in this prayer. Our heavenly Father will forgive us if we forgive those who sin against us. But if we refuse to forgive them, He will not forgive us. Matthew 6: 14 & 15. Wow! That's hard, you might say. It sure is. But when the spirit of God starts to work in us He will give us the Grace to forgive them.

I'd like to take you to the book of Galatians, Chapter 5:22. "When the Holy Spirit controls our lives HE will produce this kind of *FRUIT* in us: Love, Joy, Peace, Patience, Kindness, Goodness, Faithfulness, Gentleness and Self-control." And do you know why? Because those who belong to Christ, have nailed their natural evil desire to His Cross and crucified them there (verse 24).

WHEN DO I PRAY? It is a good question! You are on board with me here. The best time to pray is first thing in the morning. If you are a new believer I would suggest you start with 15 minutes unless of course you are led by the Holy Spirit to pray longer. The Bible says "Every morning tell him, Thank you for your kindness and every evening rejoice in all His faithfulness" (Psalms 92:2 & 3). You need to have a little bed time prayer as well. Get into the habit of reading the Bible, which is the word of God. You have to know the word of God. That means you have to get up earlier. If you honour God, God will honour you! Guaranteed! If you haven't started going to church, find a Bible preaching church and start attending Sunday services regularly. Find a group bible study to go to during the week.

PRAYING FOR A SPECIFIC NEED: Suppose you are looking for a job. You have the right qualification, a very strong resume, you have the right personality. In other words, you know pretty much you are the right candidate. So before you apply, yeah I said, *before* you even apply for the job, you pray and ask the Lord if this is from God. These are the three usual answers from God.

1. YES. Get excited and thank and praise God for the blessing. Continue to pray

for His continuous favour upon you at the work place with your co-workers, your boss and God's guidance in every area when you get the job. You are trusting God to give you this Job. Always remember to take 10% out of the gross income and take it your church to put in the offering plate. We call it 'tithe'. Tithing is a must, according to the Bible. God is saying in Malachi 3:10. "Bring all the tithes into the store house so that there will be food enough in my Temple. If you do I will open up the windows of heaven for you and pour out a blessing so great you won't have room enough to take it in".

2.   NO. When God says "NO" to a prayer request it means don't even bother thinking about it. When God closes a door nobody can open it.(Rev 3:7b) I can assure you that there will ALWAYS be the peace of God that comes with it. You might feel disappointed at first but God will bring peace to you. You will say "it's okay, I know there is something better than this coming up for me". Then you move on.

3. WAIT. Let me tell you this is not as bad as a "NO" answer. However, you have to learn to persevere or wait on the Lord. Your faith will grow and you will journey with the Holy Spirit in your walk with the Lord. You will have new experiences. You can also start to pray for and pray with others. When you bless others you will be blessed. I also recommend fasting and praying. I have mentioned some fasts in the earlier pages of the book. Pick a fast you are comfortable with. Let me also suggest you go with something that is not too easy for you. The reason being, as I mentioned earlier, fasting is not about skipping meals or not eating things that you don't like eating anyways. It's about sacrificing something you really cannot get by without. If it means something to you it will mean something to God. Don't worry about pleasing others. God sees your heart. You can do a 7 day fast or if you are led by the Holy Spirit do a 3 x 7 = 21 day fast.

Always remember if you promise God something, make sure you keep it.

The bible says that when you talk to God and vow to Him that you will do something, don't delay in doing it, for God has no pleasure in fools. Keep your promises to Him. It is far better not to say you will do something than to say you will and then not do it (Ecclesiastes 5:4 & 5).

God is Omnipotent which means He is all powerful and He has Ultimate authority over everything. The Bible says "with God everything is possible" (Matthew 19:26) When you pray for things you have to have faith in God's presence in your life and thus, in this situation. Always believe God is in control of everything, no matter how small or big the challenge is. You have to believe in God's power to do anything and everything. He can change situations supernaturally. He can go talk to people on your behalf so things will go in your favour. But the key is total trust in God like a little 4 year old child trusting their parents for everything.

FOR EFFECTIVE PRAYER

Let me give you some points to help you to have an effective prayer.

1. Always confess your sins. If there is any sin in your life Holy Spirit cannot communicate with you. You need to ask for forgiveness to people if you have issues with them.

2. Always ask in Jesus name, He is our mediator, we cannot go to God on our own. So we say I ask in Jesus name.

3. Always have faith. God honours your faith.

There are so many answered prayers throughout the Bible. I could even write a book on just the subject of "prayer". There are miracles after miracles, but there is one I want to bring up now to give you an example of answered prayer. This will help build some faith in you. It says in Joshua chapter 10, "As the men of Israel were pursuing and harassing the foe, Joshua prayed aloud, 'Let the sun stand still over Gibeon, and let the moon stand in its place over the valley of Aijalon'". The Bible says the sun and the moon didn't move until the Israeli army had finished the destruction of its enemies! So the sun stopped in the heavens and stayed there for almost 24 hours. There had never been such a day before, and there has never been another since, when the Lord stopped the sun and the moon—ALL because of ONE MAN'S PRAYER. The Lord was fighting for Israel. Have you ever heard a story like this before? I have never heard anything like this, so why did it happen? For one thing, Joshua had faith—mountain moving faith, sun and the moon stopping faith. Secondly, the bible says God was fighting for Israel, it was in God's will they should win the battle (see vs.8). Thirdly, Joshua asked the Lord to help and he prayed exactly where he wanted God to help. Always be specific when you pray. We don't need to know how God did it, He prolonged the day light so the Israelites can fight the battle and win the battle. It is God's business how He does it. Remember He is all powerful. He can do anything He wants to do. He created the heavens and the earth and everything in it. Do you know who the greatest architect is? GOD. Do you know who owns the greatest and the biggest landscaping business? GOD. Look at the beautiful world He has created with the trees, the plants, the flowers, the sea, the sandy beaches, you name it. John15:7 says, "if you stay in me and obey my commands," (whatever God tells us to do) "you may ask any request you like, and it will be granted."

HINDRANCES

1. UNFORGIVNESS is a huge barrier for hearing from God. It is not healthy at all. In fact, they say it is like we drink poison and expect the other person to die. We know it doesn't work that way. It is killing OUR body. If you need to reconcile with anyone or to make peace, you need to do it before you can get an answer from God. Sometimes it's hard to take that initiative but since you are a child of God you are expected to do it. Ask God to help you and He will definitely give you the GRACE needed to make that phone call or to send an email etc.

2. When we have wrong motives God will not answer. So always pray according to His will.

3. Idolatry. Anything or anyone above God is an idol. Is there anyone or anything you give importance to more than God?

ATTACK FROM THE ENEMY

I'd like to give you some warnings about the
attacks of the enemy (devil) on your mind.
Our mind is the first place the enemy attacks.
The devil gets a hold of our mind first, then,
he will manipulate our thoughts until we get
discouraged and depressed and give up on God.
This can lead us to get thoughts of suicide etc.
Let me make something clear here. When God
gives us an assignment that is for God's plan
and purpose, God allows the enemy to know
some of the plans God has for you. The moment
Satan finds out about it, he is trying to destroy
the plan so God's purpose won't happen. Satan
can go to people who are your friends, or even
close family, to talk to them about how to
get you out of doing this for God. Sometimes
without realizing who told them, they will in turn
approach you to convince you that what you
are going to do is not a good thing. They may
give you some reasons why it is bad for you and
your future. I call it "Satan hiding behind familiar
faces". But we have to be aware of his devices.

2 Corinthians 2:11 says to be aware of Satan's devices; we need to outsmart him. The bible talks about wearing the armor of God to fight against the plans of the enemy. Ephesians 6: 10-17 is a good portion to read to find out more about the armor. Verse 11 says "Put on the whole armor of God, that you may be able to stand against the wiles of the devil." In fact, I think you should read the whole chapter to get more understanding of things. What the Apostle Paul is saying is, that our strength must come from the Lord's mighty power in us. We need to know the word of God and pray earnestly for the needs that are in God's plan, as we pray for others too.

A while ago one morning, since I started writing this book, I had a severe attack form the enemy which I must say I hadn't had in a long, long time. It was BAD! I did my morning prayers as usual, and around 9am I had a severe attack from the enemy. It was a comment made by somebody. I thought I should pray and rebuke the enemy, but I didn't feel like praying. I was even thinking, "what's the point of all this?" My mind was already having negative thoughts. I knew for sure this was from the enemy and I looked for some kind of encouragement from another believer. I'm telling you, the attack was so strong that, when I turned the TV on to the Christian Channel to get some support by listening to someone's encouraging message, guess what? They were showing part of a church service where they were praying the prayers by repeating after and responding to the minister, as I did in the main line church I attended when growing up, except they were praying to Mary, the mother of Jesus. I went to a catholic school where they prayed to Mary, mother of Jesus, which, later on in my life I was shown is the wrong way to pray. Mary is a very Blessed woman. God chose her to be the earthly mother of Jesus. But praying to her is idol worship. On that note, I want to add that we don't pray to angels either. We don't worship them or pray to them. It's okay to have those little porcelain figurines in your curio cabinet or show case. Dust them and keep them clean that's it. Now believe this. The attack was so overpowering that when I saw the whole congregation praying to Mary I began to wonder after all these years what I had originally believed was the right thing to do. I was feeling so depressed, and I put my head down, sitting on my sofa thinking about what the next step is here. I thought maybe I should go to the computer and look at what I was writing. Maybe when I read some of my life experiences I would feel encouraged. I went over and turned it on but the internet was down. I said "I want everything God promised. I'm taking back everything the devil stole from me." I kept saying "God will give me JOY instead of discouragement and PRAISE instead of heaviness. I have made up my mind not to yield to the defeat that the enemy is planning." I decided to wait for the next program on TV which I usually watch at that time of the morning. I listened to the first 20 minutes but it wasn't very convincing. As I watched the next one, the Spirit of God started to work in my heart and mind. What the minister was talking about was **exactly** what was going on in my spirit. I knew it was a test because God sometimes allows the enemy to attack His children. About an hour later, I was back to my normal self again. Praise the Lord!

They are 2 reasons I'm telling you this story.

1. Anybody can get attacked by the enemy, and most of the time we can rebuke the enemy by ourselves, but other times we need the help of a trustworthy friend or another believer to pray with us. I want to add that sometimes God *allows* the enemy to do it, but even then remember God is with us and His angels are

protecting us. Joshua 1: 9 says (Living Bible) "Be bold and strong! Banish fear and doubt! For remember, the Lord your God is with you wherever you go." God gave Joshua an assignment and along with that God is giving him instructions and ends with that encouraging verse; A PROMISE (Joshua 1:9).

2. To strengthen our own faith and to have a testimony for others who are in need of some uplifting and encouragement. God wants us to tell others about the good things we receive from our Heavenly Father to honour Him and to praise Him. That is part of our Thanksgiving. Always remember to give Him Thanks & Praise. That is expected of us. I personally like testimonies because it is our own experiences we're sharing with others. That is the best way to get the attention of a person needing help! It's first hand information. We went through it ourselves and we are telling our own story, as opposed to listening to Billy talking about Johnny's trial. That's good too, but a personal testimony is much more effective.

MEEKNESS IS NOT WEAKNESS

As a child of God, a true follower of Jesus, we are expected to be humble. It takes strength to be humble. Think about life's situations, in our interaction with others. Isn't it easier to yell and shout back when others are mean to us? It takes lot of will power and strength to be quiet or respond calmly. In the book of Proverbs 15:1 (this is my personal slogan) it says, "a soft answer turns away wrath, but harsh words cause quarrels."

CONCLUSION

My prayer is that this book will help you to commit, re-commit your life to Jesus, and have a rewarding, enjoyable journey with the Lord while you are on this earth.

XOXO

ABOUT THE AUTHOR

I was born and raised in a Christian home. My ancestors were Christians for generations. I am a university graduate, majored in Economics. I had all plans to become a successful Entrepreneur on my own and marry later on, and expand or create an empire with the man someday I would marry. I wanted a large family, lot of children. I grew up in a large family. But destiny took me in a different direction. I am now a single woman. I am involved in the ministry of my church I attend. I have led the Singles Ministry of my church for 7 years and also did a Bible study. I still do a Bible study. I have two adult children from my marriage. They are both done their College/University studies and are presently working.